D1272430

CHILDREN'S AUTHORS

DAV PILKEY

Jill C. Wheeler
ABDO Publishing Company

visit us at
www.abdopublishing.com

Published by ABDO Publishing Company, PO Box 398166, Minneapolis, Minnesota 55439.
Copyright © 2013 by Abdo Consulting Group, Inc. International copyrights reserved in all
countries. No part of this book may be reproduced in any form without written permission from the
publisher. The Checkerboard Library™ is a trademark and logo of ABDO Publishing Company.

Printed in the United States of America, North Mankato, Minnesota.
102012
012013

 PRINTED ON RECYCLED PAPER

Cover Photo: Vernon Area Public Library
Interior Photos: AP Images p. 11; iStockphoto p. 7; Copyright © Scholastic Inc.
    Reprinted by permission. pp. 9, 13, 15, 17, 19; Vernon Area Public Library pp. 5, 21

Series Coordinator: Megan M. Gunderson
Editors: Tamara L. Britton, Stephanie Hedlund
Art Direction: Neil Klinepier

Special thanks to Anna Libra for her invaluable assistance with this project.

Cataloging-in-Publication Data

Wheeler, Jill C., 1964-
 Dav Pilkey / Jill C. Wheeler.
  p. cm. -- (Children's authors)
Includes bibliographical references and index.
ISBN 978-1-61783-577-3
1. Pilkey, Dav, 1966- --Juvenile literature. 2. Authors, American--20th century--Biography--
Juvenile literature. 3. Children's stories--Authorship--Juvenile literature.   I. Title.
818/.5209-dc23   5927734
[B]
                                                                    2012946383

CONTENTS

THE MAN BEHIND THE CAPTAIN

Most students try to avoid imagining their principal in his or her underwear. Fortunately for many readers, Dav Pilkey did not!

Pilkey is the author and illustrator of the popular Captain Underpants series. Since 1997, these books have sold more than 50 million copies in the United States alone. In addition, several of the titles have **debuted** at the top of best-seller lists.

Readers appreciate that Pilkey writes and draws what he knows. When Pilkey was in first grade, doctors diagnosed him with **ADHD**. The heroes of his Captain Underpants books have ADHD as well. Yet that has not stopped the heroic fourth graders from saving the world!

Pilkey is also the creator of the Dumb Bunnies, Big Dog and Little Dog, and Dragon book series. For a kid whose classmates called him "David Puke-ey," Dav Pilkey has come a very long way.

Dav can be pronounced like "Dave" or like "have."

DAV WITH NO E

Dav Pilkey was born David Murray Pilkey Jr. on March 4, 1966, in Cleveland, Ohio. Originally, his name was spelled Dave. He began spelling his name without the final *e* in 1983. At the time, Dav was a waiter at Pizza Hut. There, the name tag label maker misspelled his name. The new spelling stuck.

Dav's father, David Pilkey Sr., was a steel sales manager. His mother, Barbara Pembridge Pilkey, was an organist at a local church. Dav grew up with an older sister named Cindy.

Dav does not remember much about his very early childhood. However, his parents tell him that he was nearly always happy. As an infant, he laughed all the time. He even laughed in his sleep!

Dav was an extremely active child. He was diagnosed with **ADHD** after setting the record for the most time spent in the principal's office. He also held the school record of sticking the most crayons up his nose at one time. He fit six!

Cleveland is a port city on Lake Erie and the Cuyahoga River.

Hallway Artist

In Elyria, Ohio, Dav attended a **strict parochial** school. Yet he often acted out in class. As the class clown, he did and said things to make other students laugh. However, Dav's teachers did not appreciate his humor. In fact, his second grade teacher often sent him to the hallway to punish him.

This happened so many times that Dav had his own desk there. Every day, he would stock it with paper, pencils, and crayons. Alone in the hallway, he drew and made up stories about superheroes. He stapled pages together to create his own comic books.

Dav needed a name for his creation. One day, his teacher had said the word *underpants* in class. The students laughed, and the teacher became upset. She told the class that underwear was not funny. But Dav disagreed! He named his superhero "The Amazing Captain Underpants."

Dav's classmates found his comic books very funny. Yet one of his teachers ripped up his drawings. He told Dav he needed to take life more seriously. Dav ignored this negative advice.

Luckily, Dav's parents always supported him. When Dav was not drawing in the hallway, he was often drawing at home. Other kids were outside playing football and baseball. But Dav was inside drawing animals, monsters, and superheroes.

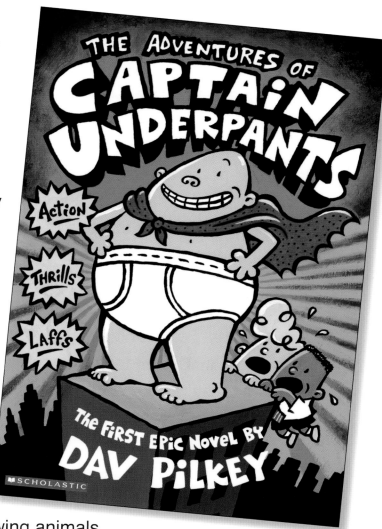

As a kid, Dav wrote books his classmates read. Today, his books are published in 19 countries!

PUBLISHED!

Dav's unpleasant elementary school experience was nothing compared to high school. There, teachers tried to talk him out of a career as an artist. One time, his principal personally took Dav out of class to tell him that he was not special. He added that Dav would never make enough money just by drawing.

Even so, Dav decided to pursue art as a career. He headed to Kent State University in Kent, Ohio, in 1984. He **majored** in art. There, one of Dav's English teachers finally appreciated his creative writing skills. In fact, the teacher encouraged him to write a book.

This time, Dav listened. He began writing and illustrating his first book, *World War Won*. It is the story of two animal kingdoms fighting for power. Dav entered the **manuscript** in the National Written and Illustrated By... contest. Dav won

Dav graduated from Kent State with an Associate of Arts degree in 1987.

for his age group! This meant that at age 20, he would be a published author.

After this success, Dav began to research children's books. He read everything he could by all of his favorite authors. These included Arnold Lobel, James Marshall, and Harry Allard. He read them over and over to figure out what makes a good book good.

Dragons and Bunnies

After college, Pilkey worked in Ohio as a **freelance** artist. He illustrated other people's books. Then in 1991, the first two books in his Dragon series were published. The series features a lovable blue dragon who winds up in funny situations. Just two years later, Pilkey followed an actual dream he'd had. He moved from Ohio to Oregon.

In 1994, Pilkey's next series was published. The Dumb Bunnies books feature a family of not-too-bright animals. The stories are based on famous fairy tales, such as "The Three Bears" and "Little Red Riding Hood." The Dumb Bunnies series was published under the **pseudonym** Sue Denim. Pilkey's joke was that *pseudonym* is pronounced like "Sue Denim."

Pilkey did not write only funny books. His book *The Paperboy* is the story of a young African-American paperboy and his dog. The pair rise before dawn, deliver papers, and

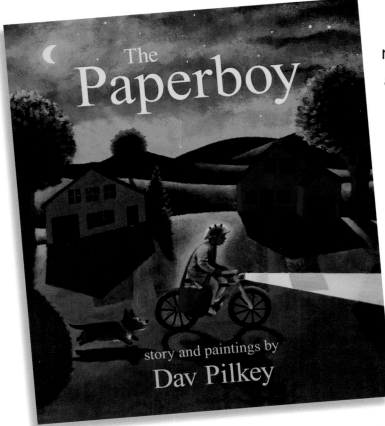

return home to dream about flying across the sky. *The Paperboy* was named a **Caldecott Honor Book** in 1997.

For very young children, Pilkey wrote the Big Dog and Little Dog series. Pilkey got the idea for them after joking about dog stories with a friend. He realized that these stories would make good books for toddlers. So, the pictures are big and the pages are thick cardboard. Kids enjoyed these stories about two dogs who play in puddles and go on walks.

Pre-shrunk and Cottony

For his next project, Pilkey thought back to his school days. Growing up, Pilkey hated reading. So when a teacher assigned a book for class, he looked for three things. First, the book had to have large type. That meant there would be less to read. Next, the book needed to have short chapters. Finally, any book that caught his eye had to have pictures.

Big type, short chapters, and pictures were all easy to create. But there was still something missing. The former class clown quickly added the last piece. Whatever Pilkey was going to write had to be funny. Fortunately, he remembered Captain Underpants.

The Captain Underpants series features two fourth graders named George Beard and Harold Hutchins. They **hypnotize** their school principal and turn him into a superhero. As Captain Underpants, he wears nothing but white briefs and a cape! George and Harold make him take on bank robbers, evil scientists, and other criminals.

Pilkey knew he was writing for kids who adored a good potty joke. Even as an adult, those jokes still make him laugh. So slowly, villains with names like "Professor Poopypants" were created. Yet they were always beaten by Captain Underpants. He stands for "Truth, Justice, and ALL that is Pre-shrunk and Cottony."

Funny and Cool

The Adventures of Captain Underpants: An Epic Novel was published in September 1997. Almost immediately, readers could not get enough of their new favorite superhero. He caught the attention of kids who had not been reading much before. So teachers took notice, too.

Pilkey says his books are appealing because they are funny and simple. Even the misspelled words add to the story. Pilkey says his childhood spelling had mistakes. So, it makes sense that his characters should make spelling errors as well. He hopes kids realize it's easier to be creative if they're not worried about making mistakes.

Pilkey also gives his readers variety. Some chapters are only one or two pages long. They all have silly pictures. Some are made up of comic books. Others are flip-pages. And, Pilkey doesn't work in just one **medium**. He creates art with watercolors, colored pencils, **acrylics**, markers, and **collage**.

In 2002, Pilkey switched things up again. This time, he had George and Harold write their own book as a class project. It is the story of a baby who lands in superpower juice. He becomes a crime-fighting sensation. The story is the start of Pilkey's Super Diaper Baby series.

The first Super Diaper Baby e-books were released in 2012.

STINKY SCIENCE FICTION

Next, Pilkey took on the **genre** of science fiction. He introduced his fans to a heroic mouse named Ricky Ricotta. Ricky befriends a giant robot. The two take on everything from massive mosquitoes to stinky litterbugs. Pilkey had seven Ricky Ricotta books published between 2000 and 2005.

In 1999, Pilkey had moved to a small island in Washington. There, he and his dog Little Dog's favorite activity was to eat at the local sushi restaurant. Pilkey would eat vegetarian sushi rolls. And the owner, Sayuri, would make a special meal for Little Dog. Sayuri and Pilkey fell in love and were married on a beach under a full moon in 2005.

That same year, Pilkey began working on a new book. At first, the story was about caveman paramedics. Eventually, it turned into one about kung-fu cavemen.

Pilkey believes that's the funny thing about letting characters stay in a writer's head for years. They begin to live on their own and create their own stories. They change over time! *The Adventures of Ook and Gluk: Kung-Fu Cavemen from the Future* was published in May 2011.

★RICKY RICOTTA'S★
MIGHTY ROBOT

with FLIP-O-RAMA action scenes

MORE THAN A MILLION RICKY RICOTTA BOOKS IN PRINT!

the first adventure novel by Dav Pilkey
pictures by Martin Ontiveros

ORIGINALLY PUBLISHED AS RICKY RICOTTA'S GIANT ROBOT

SIMPLY SHOCKING

Pilkey has written and illustrated more than 45 books. He has won a **Caldecott Honor**. Yet he is still best known for the doodles he started in the hallway of his elementary school.

Unfortunately, not everyone was thrilled about a superhero who gives wedgies to bad guys. The principal of a Connecticut elementary school felt that the Captain Underpants books were causing problems. So, the books were banned. Yet none of this affects their popularity.

Captain Underpants also caught the attention of movie makers. In 2011, DreamWorks Animation announced plans to make a Captain Underpants film. Originally, Pilkey was worried that a movie might not tell the same story of morality and responsibility as the books. However, he changed his mind after seeing *How to Train Your Dragon* and *Kung Fu Panda*.

Pilkey had taken a break from writing to care for his father, who died 2008. Then in January 2012, Pilkey's publisher announced that Captain Underpants would be back. Two new books would be released in 2012 and 2013. Fans can't wait to see what Pilkey has Captain Underpants do next!

Pilkey traveled the country to sign his new book in 2012.

GLOSSARY

acrylics - certain paints used by artists.

ADHD - attention deficit/hyperactivity disorder. A mental disorder involving restlessness and being unable to concentrate.

Caldecott Honor Book - a runner-up to the Caldecott Medal. The Caldecott Medal is an award the American Library Association gives to the artist who illustrated the year's best picture book.

collage (kuh-LAHZH) - art composed of a variety of materials, such as paper and cloth, glued onto a surface.

debut (DAY-byoo) - to first appear.

freelance - relating to an artist or author without a long-term commitment to a single employer.

genre (ZHAHN-ruh) - a type of art, music, or literature.

hypnotize - to cause hypnosis, which is similar to deep sleep. A person under hypnosis will readily do what the person who hypnotized him or her suggests.

major - to study a particular subject or field.

manuscript - a handwritten or typed book or article not yet published.

medium - a means of artistic expression or communication.

parochial (puh-ROH-kee-uhl) - of or relating to a church.

pseudonym (SOO-duh-nihm) - a name used by a writer instead of his or her own real name.

strict - following or demanding others to follow rules or regulations in a rigid, exact manner.

WEB SITES

To learn more about Dav Pilkey, visit ABDO Publishing Company online. Web sites about Dav Pilkey are featured on our Book Links page. These links are routinely monitored and updated to provide the most current information available.

www.abdopublishing.com

INDEX

EMMA S. CLARK MEMORIAL LIBRARY

SETAUKET, NEW YORK 11733

To view your account,

renew or request an item,

visit www.emmaclark.org